TO

Brandon Poelstra

FROM

Cornerstone AWANA

FAMILY
CHRISTIAN
PRESS

THE REAL SERIES

MAKING
REAL GOOD
CHOICES

30 DEVOTIONS

The quoted ideas expressed in this book (but not scripture verses) are not, in all cases, exact quotations, as some have been edited for clarity and brevity. In all cases, the author has attempted to maintain the speaker's original intent. In some cases, quoted material for this book was obtained from secondary sources, primarily print media. While every effort was made to ensure the accuracy of these sources, the accuracy cannot be guaranteed. For additions, deletions, corrections or clarifications in future editions of this text, please write FAMILY CHRISTIAN PRESS.

Scripture quotations are taken from:

The Holy Bible, King James Version

The Holy Bible, New International Version (NIV) Copyright © 1973, 1978, 1984, by International Bible Society. Used by permission of Zondervan Publishing House. All rights reserved.

The New American Standard Bible®, (NASB) Copyright © 1960, 1962, 1963, 1968, 1971, 1972, 1973, 1975, 1977, 1995 by The Lockman Foundation. Used by permission.

The Holy Bible, New King James Version (NKJV) Copyright © 1982 by Thomas Nelson, Inc. Used by permission.

The Holy Bible, New Living Translation, (NLT) Copyright © 1996. Used by permission of Tyndale House Publishers, Inc., Wheaton, Illinois 60189. All rights reserved.

New Century Version®. (NCV) Copyright © 1987, 1988, 1991 by Word Publishing, a division of Thomas Nelson, Inc. All rights reserved. Used by permission.

The Message (MSG) This edition issued by contractual arrangement with NavPress, a division of The Navigators, U.S.A. Originally published by NavPress in English as THE MESSAGE: The Bible in Contemporary Language copyright 2002-2003 by Eugene Peterson. All rights reserved.

The Holman Christian Standard Bible™ (HCSB) Copyright © 1999, 2000, 2001 by Holman Bible Publishers. Used by permission.

Cover Design by Kim Russell / Wahoo Designs
Page Layout by Bart Dawson

ISBN 1-58334-335-0

Printed in the United States of America

MAKING REAL GOOD CHOICES

30 DEVOTIONS

Table of Contents

Introduction

Choices—you've already made millions of them, and you've still got millions more to make. Most of these choices, of course, are of the smaller variety—like what to do at a given moment or what to say or what to wear or how to direct your thoughts. A few of your choices will be big league decisions, like choosing to be a Christian or choosing a profession or choosing a spouse. But whatever choices you face, whether they're big, little, or somewhere in between, you can be sure that the quality of your choices will make a huge difference in the quality of your life.

Are you facing some difficult decisions? Are you seeking to change some aspect of your life? Do you desire the eternal abundance and peace that can be yours through Christ? If so, this book is intended to help. It contains 30 devotional readings, one for each day of the month. And make no mistake about it: the principles contained in this text can help you make smarter choices, choices that will be pleasing to you and to God. So do yourself a favor by taking these ideas seriously. When you do, you'll start making choices that will improve your day and your life.

CHAPTER 1

Your Choices Can Make a Really Big Difference!

I am offering you life or death, blessings or curses. Now, choose life! . . . To choose life is to love the Lord your God, obey him, and stay close to him.

Deuteronomy 30:19-20 NCV

hoices, choices, choices! You've got so many choices to make, and sometimes, making those choices isn't easy. At times you're torn between what you want to do and what you ought to do. When that happens, it's up to you to choose wisely . . . or else!

The choices that you make today can make a really big difference in the quality of your life now and in the future. When you make wise choices, you are rewarded; when you make unwise choices, you must accept the consequences. It's as simple as that. So make sure that your choices are pleasing to God . . . or else!

The Basics:
What You Need to Know

First you make choices . . . and pretty soon
those choices begin to shape your life.
That's why you must make smart choices . . .
or face the consequences of making dumb ones.

What the Bible Says

*The thing you should want most is God's kingdom
and doing what God wants. Then all these
other things you need will be given to you.*

Matthew 6:33 NCV

*So I strive always to keep my conscience
clear before God and man.*

Acts 24:16 NIV

*If you don't know what you're doing, pray to
the Father. He loves to help. You'll get his help,
and won't be condescended to when you ask for it.
Ask boldly, believingly, without a second thought.
People who "worry their prayers" are like wind-whipped
waves. Don't think you're going to get anything
from the Master that way, adrift at sea,
keeping all your options open.*

James 1:5-8 MSG

Big Ideas

Commitment to His lordship on Easter, at revivals,
or even every Sunday is not enough. We must choose
this day—and every day—whom we will serve.
This deliberate act of the will is the inevitable choice
between habitual fellowship and habitual failure.

Beth Moore

Life is a series of choices between the bad,
the good, and the best.
Everything depends on how we choose.

Vance Havner

No matter how many books you read,
no matter how many schools you attend,
you're never really wise until you
start making wise choices.

Marie T. Freeman

A Prayer for Today

Lord, help me to make choices that are pleasing to You. Help me to be honest, patient, and kind. And above all, help me to follow the teachings of Jesus, not just today, but every day.

Amen

CHAPTER 2

The Choice to Put God First

You shall have no other gods before Me.
Exodus 20:3 NKJV

ho is in charge of your heart? Is it God, or is it something else? Have you given Christ your heart, your soul, your talents, your time, and your testimony? Or are you giving Him little more than a few hours each Sunday morning?

In the book of Exodus, God warns that we should place no gods before Him. Yet all too often, we place our Lord in second, third, or fourth place as we worship other things. When we unwittingly place possessions or relationships above our love for the Creator, we create big problems for ourselves.

Have you chosen to allow God to rule your heart? Make certain that the honest answer to this question is a resounding yes. In the life of every thoughtful believer, God comes first. And that's precisely the place that He deserves in your heart.

The Basics:
What You Need to Know

If you don't choose to put God first,
you're making a bad choice.

What the Bible Says

He that loveth not, knoweth not God;
for God is love.
1 John 4:8 KJV

No one has seen God, ever. But if we love one another,
God dwells deeply within us, and his love becomes
complete in us—perfect love! This is how we know
we're living steadily and deeply in him, and he in us:
He's given us life from his life, from his very own Spirit.
1 John 4:12-13 MSG

Yet, O LORD, you are our Father.
We are the clay, you are the potter;
we are all the work of your hand.
Isaiah 64:8 NIV

Big Ideas

God is the beyond in the midst of our life.

Dietrich Bonhoeffer

There is a God shaped vacuum in the heart
of every man which cannot be filled by
any created thing, but only by God,
the Creator, made known through Jesus.

Blaise Pascal

One with God is a majority.

Billy Graham

A Prayer for Today

Dear Lord, thank You for all the blessings
You have given me. Today and every day
I will do my best to please You by thinking
good thoughts and doing good deeds.
Amen

CHAPTER 3

You're Worth It!

*You're blessed when you're content with
just who you are—no more, no less.
That's the moment you find yourselves proud owners
of everything that can't be bought.*
Matthew 5:5 MSG

ow many people in the world are exactly like you? The only person in the world who's exactly like you . . . IS YOU! And that means you're special: special to God, special to your family, special to your friends, and a special addition to God's wonderful world!

But sometimes, when you're tired, angry, dejected, or depressed, you may not feel very special. In fact, you may decide that you're the ugliest duckling in the pond, a not-very-special person . . . but whenever you think like that, you're mistaken.

The Bible says that God made you in "an amazing and wonderful way." So the next time that you start feeling like you don't measure up, remember this: when God made all the people of the earth, He only made one you. You're incredibly valuable to God, and that means you should think of yourself as a V.I.P. (A Very Important Person). God wants you to have the best, and you deserve the best . . . you're worth it!

The Basics:
What You Need to Know

You're an amazing person, created by God,
and you deserve the best from life.
Wise choices can help you earn the biggest rewards.

What the Bible Says

God began doing a good work in you,
and I am sure he will continue it until it is finished
when Jesus Christ comes again.

Philippians 1:6 NCV

For you made us only a little lower than God,
and you crowned us with glory and honor.

Psalm 8:5 NLT

You made my whole being . . . I praise you
because you made me in an amazing and
wonderful way. What you have done
is wonderful. I know this very well.

Psalm 139:13-14 NCV

Big Ideas

Human worth does not depend on beauty or
intelligence or accomplishments. We are all more
valuable than the possessions of the entire world
simply because God gave us that value.

James Dobson

Being loved by Him whose opinion
matters most gives us the security
to risk loving, too—even loving ourselves.

Gloria Gaither

You are valuable just because you exist.
Not because of what you do or what you have done,
but simply because you are.

Max Lucado

A Prayer for Today

Dear Lord, keep me mindful that I am
a special person, created by You, loved by You,
and saved by Your Son.
Amen

CHAPTER 4

Choosing Your Thoughts

There is one thing I always do. Forgetting the past and straining toward what is ahead, I keep trying to reach the goal and get the prize for which God called me . . . .
Philippians 3:13-14 NCV

here does a good attitude begin? It starts in our hearts and works its way out from there. Jesus taught us that a pure heart is a wonderful blessing. It's up to each of us to fill our hearts with love for God, love for Jesus, and love for all people. When we do, good things happen.

Sometimes, of course, we don't feel much like feeling good. Sometimes, when we're tired or frustrated or angry, we simply don't want to have a good attitude. On those days when we're feeling bad, it's time to calm down . . . and rest up.

Do you want to be the best person you can be? Then you shouldn't grow tired of doing the right things . . . and you shouldn't ever grow tired of thinking the right thoughts.

The Basics:
What You Need to Know

You have the power to choose the direction
of your thoughts. Good thoughts lead to good results;
bad thoughts lead elsewhere.

What the Bible Says

For the word of God is living and active.
Sharper than any double-edged sword,
it penetrates even to dividing soul and spirit,
joints and marrow; it judges the thoughts
and attitudes of the heart.

Hebrews 4:12 NIV

A miserable heart means a miserable life;
a cheerful heart fills the day with a song.

Proverbs 15:15 MSG

Therefore, since Christ suffered in his body,
arm yourselves also with the same attitude, because
he who has suffered in his body is done with sin.
As a result, he does not live the rest of his earthly life
for evil human desires, but rather for the will of God.

1 Peter 4:1-2 NIV

Big Ideas

The Reference Point for the Christian is the Bible.
All values, judgments, and attitudes must be
gauged in relationship to this Reference Point.

Ruth Bell Graham

You've heard the saying, "Life is what you make it."
That means we have a choice. We can choose to have
a life full of frustration and fear, but we can just as
easily choose one of joy and contentment.

Dennis Swanberg

We are either the masters or the victims of our attitudes.
It is a matter of personal choice. Who we are today
is the result of choices we made yesterday.
Tomorrow, we will become what we choose today.
To change means to choose to change.

John Maxwell

A Prayer for Today

Lord, I pray for an attitude that is Christlike.
Whatever my situation, whether good or bad,
happy or sad, let me respond with an attitude
of optimism, faith, and love for You.
Amen

CHAPTER 5

Trying to Please Too Many People Can Lead to Big Trouble

My son, if sinners entice you, don't be persuaded.
Proverbs 1:10 HCSB

Are you a people-pleaser or a God-pleaser? Hopefully, you're far more concerned with pleasing God than you are with pleasing your friends. But face facts: even if you're a devoted Christian, you're still going to feel the urge to impress your friends and acquaintances—and sometimes that urge will be strong.

Peer pressure can be good or bad, depending upon who your peers are and how they behave. If your friends encourage you to follow God's will and to obey His commandments, then you'll experience positive peer pressure, and that's a good thing. But, if your friends encourage you to do foolish things, then you're facing a different kind of peer pressure . . . and you'd better beware.

To sum it up, here's your choice: you can choose to please God first, or you can fall victim to peer pressure. The choice is yours—and so are the consequences.

The Basics:
What You Need to Know

If you try too hard to please other people
(instead of trying to please God),
you may find yourself making unwise choices.

What the Bible Says

Friend, don't go along with evil. Model the good.
The person who does good does God's work.
The person who does evil falsifies God,
doesn't know the first thing about God.
3 John 1:11 MSG

Don't become partners with those who reject God.
How can you make a partnership out of
right and wrong? That's not partnership;
that's war. Is light best friends with dark?
2 Corinthians 6:14 MSG

We must obey God rather than men.
Acts 5:29 HCSB

Big Ideas

If you choose to awaken a passion for God,
you will have to choose your friends wisely.

Lisa Bevere

Those who follow the crowd usually get lost in it.

Rick Warren

Do you want to be wise?
Choose wise friends.

Charles Swindoll

A Prayer for Today

Dear Lord, other people may want me to misbehave,
but You want me to behave myself.
And that's what I want, too—I want to do what's right.
So help me do the right thing, Lord,
even when it's hard.
Amen

CHAPTER 6

Making the Choice to Read God's Book

You will be a good servant of Christ Jesus, constantly nourished on the words of the faith and of the sound doctrine which you have been following.

1 Timothy 4:6 NASB

o you read your Bible a lot . . . or not? The answer to this simple question will determine, to a surprising extent, the quality of your decisions, the quality of your life, and the direction of your faith.

You (and only you) must decide whether God's Word will be a bright spotlight that guides your path every day or a tiny nightlight that occasionally flickers in the dark. The decision to study the Bible—or not—is an important choice; how you choose to use your Bible will have a profound impact on your future.

The Bible is unlike any other book. It is a priceless gift from your Creator, a tool that God intends for you to use in every aspect of your life. And, it contains promises upon which you, as a Christian, can and must depend.

God's Word can be a roadmap to success and spiritual abundance. Make it your roadmap. God's wisdom can be a light to guide your steps. Claim it as your light today, tomorrow, and every day of your life—and then walk confidently in the footsteps of God's only begotten Son.

The Basics:
What You Need to Know

If you want to know God, you should take time
to read the book He wrote.

What the Bible Says

There's nothing like the written Word of God for showing you the way to salvation through faith in Christ Jesus. Every part of Scripture is God-breathed and useful one way or another, showing us truth, exposing our rebellion, correcting our mistakes, training us to live God's way. Through the Word we are put together and shaped up for the tasks God has for us.

2 Timothy 3:15-17 MSG

But grow in the grace and knowledge of
our Lord and Savior Jesus Christ.
To Him be the glory both now and forever. Amen.

2 Peter 3:18 NKJV

For I am not ashamed of the gospel of Christ,
for it is the power of God to salvation
for everyone who believes.

Romans 1:16 NKJV

Big Ideas

We can't stand before God on the day of judgment
and explain that our incredible ignorance is
our pastor's fault. It is our responsibility to
access God's Word for ourselves.

Sheila Walsh

Some read the Bible to learn, and some
read the Bible to hear from heaven.

Andrew Murray

Only through routine, regular exposure to
God's Word can you and I draw out the nutrition
needed to grow a heart of faith.

Elizabeth George

A Prayer for Today

Dear Lord, I praise You for Your Holy Word.
Let the Bible be my guide for life here on earth
and for life eternal. And, let me be a worthy example
to others, Lord, so that they might see my love
for You reflected in everything that I say and do.
Amen

CHAPTER 7

Making the Choice to Follow Jesus

*Then he told them what they could expect
for themselves: "Anyone who intends
to come with me has to let me lead."*
Luke 9:23 MSG

With whom will you choose to walk today? Will you walk with shortsighted people who honor the ways of the world, or will you walk with the Son of God? Jesus walks with you. Are you walking with Him? Hopefully, you will choose to walk with Him today and every day of your life.

Jesus has called upon believers of every generation (and that includes you) to follow in His footsteps. And God's Word promises that when you follow in Christ's footsteps, you will learn how to live freely and lightly (Matthew 11:28-30).

Jesus doesn't want you to be a run-of-the-mill, follow-the-crowd kind of person. Jesus wants you to be a "new creation" through Him. And that's exactly what you should want for yourself, too. Nothing is more important than your wholehearted commitment to your Creator and to His only begotten Son. Your faith must never be an afterthought; it must be your ultimate priority, your ultimate possession, and your ultimate passion.

You are the recipient of Christ's love. Accept it enthusiastically and share it passionately. Jesus deserves your extreme enthusiasm; the world deserves it; and you deserve the experience of sharing it.

The Basics:
What You Need to Know

If you choose to follow Jesus,
you'll be eternally grateful that you did.

What the Bible Says

No one can serve two masters.
Either he will hate the one and love the other,
or he will be devoted to the one and despise the other.

Matthew 6:24 NIV

I've laid down a pattern for you.
What I've done, you do.

John 13:15 MSG

Whoever is not willing to carry the cross and follow me
is not worthy of me. Those who try to hold on to their
lives will give up true life. Those who give up
their lives for me will hold on to true life.

Matthew 10:38-39 NCV

Big Ideas

Our responsibility is to feed from Him, to stay close to
Him, to follow Him—because sheep easily go astray—
so that we eternally experience the protection and
companionship of our Great Shepherd
the Lord Jesus Christ.

Franklin Graham

So Christ is an ever-flowing fountain; he is continually
supplying his people, and the fountain is not spent.
They who live upon Christ may have fresh supplies from
him for all eternity; they may have an increase
of blessedness that is new, and new still,
and which never will come to an end.

Jonathan Edwards

Will you, with a glad and eager surrender,
hand yourself and all that concerns you over into
his hands? If you will do this, your soul will begin to
know something of the joy of union with Christ.

Hannah Whitall Smith

A Prayer for Today

Dear Lord, You sent Jesus to save the world
and to save me. I thank You for Jesus,
and I will do my best to follow Him,
today and forever.
Amen

CHAPTER 8

Choosing the Right Crowd

Greater love has no one than this,
that he lay down his life for his friends.

John 15:13 NIV

ecause we tend to become like our friends, we must choose our friends carefully. Because our friends influence us in ways that are both subtle and powerful, we must ensure that our friendships honor God. Because our friends have the power to lift us up or to bring us down, we must select friends who, by their words and their actions, encourage us to lead Christ-centered lives.

When we build lasting friendships that are pleasing to God, we are blessed. When we seek out encouraging friends and mentors, they lift us up. And, when we make ourselves a powerful source of encouragement to others, we do God's work here on earth.

Do you seek to be a godly Christian? If so, you should build friendships that honor your Creator. When you do, God will bless you and your friends, today and forever.

The Basics:
What You Need to Know

You'll probably end up behaving like
your friends behave . . . and if that's a scary thought,
it time to make a new set of friends.

What the Bible Says

A friend loves you all the time,
and a brother helps in time of trouble.
Proverbs 17:17 NCV

Do not be deceived:
"Bad company corrupts good morals."
1 Corinthians 15:33 HCSB

As iron sharpens iron, a friend sharpens a friend.
Proverbs 27:17 NLT

Big Ideas

The best times in life are made a thousand times better
when shared with a dear friend.

Luci Swindoll

God has not called us to see through each other,
but to see each other through.

Jess Moody

Yes, the Spirit was sent to be our Counselor.
Yes, Jesus speaks to us personally.
But often he works through another human being.

John Eldredge

A Prayer for Today

Lord, thank You for my friends.
Let me be a trustworthy friend to others,
and let my love for You be reflected
in my genuine love for them.
Amen

CHAPTER 9

Wise Choices 101

Do not deceive yourselves. If any one of you thinks he is wise by the standards of this age, he should become a "fool" so that he may become wise. For the wisdom of this world is foolishness in God's sight.

1 Corinthians 3:18-19 NIV

ecause you're a student, your head is undoubtedly filled with valuable information. But, there is much yet to learn. Wisdom is like a savings account: If you add to it consistently, then eventually you'll have a great sum. The secret to success is consistency.

Would you like to be wise? Then keep learning. Seek wisdom every day, and seek it in the right place. That place, of course, is, first and foremost, the Word of God. And remember this: it's not enough to simply read God's Word; you've also got to live by it.

The Basics:
What You Need to Know

Simply put, wisdom starts with God.
If you don't have God's wisdom—
and if you don't live according to God's rules—
you'll pay a big price later.

What the Bible Says

Wisdom is the principal thing; therefore get wisdom.
And in all your getting, get understanding.
Proverbs 4:7 NKJV

The Lord says, "I will make you wise and show you
where to go. I will guide you and watch over you."
Psalm 32:8 NCV

Happy is the person who finds wisdom,
the one who gets understanding.
Proverbs 3:13 NCV

Big Ideas

Wisdom is the right use of knowledge.
To know is not to be wise. Many men know a great
deal, and are all the greater fools for it. But to know
how to use knowledge is to have wisdom.

C. H. Spurgeon

If we neglect the Bible, we cannot expect
to benefit from the wisdom and direction that
result from knowing God's Word.

Vonette Bright

Don't expect wisdom to come into your life like great
chunks of rock on a conveyor belt. Wisdom comes
privately from God as a byproduct of right decisions,
godly reactions, and the application of spiritual
principles to daily circumstances.

Charles Swindoll

A Prayer for Today

Lord, when I trust in the wisdom of the world,
I will sometimes be led astray, but when I trust in
Your wisdom, I build my life on a firm foundation.
Today and every day I will trust Your Word and follow it,
knowing that the ultimate wisdom is Your wisdom
and the ultimate truth is Your truth.
Amen

CHAPTER 10

Choosing a Healthy Lifestyle

*Don't you know that you are God's sanctuary
and that the Spirit of God lives in you?*
1 Corinthians 3:16 HCSB

aintaining good health is not only a common-sense exercise in personal discipline, it is also a spiritual journey ordained by our Creator. God does not intend that we abuse bodies by giving in to excessive appetites or to lazy behavior. To the contrary, God instructs us to protect our physical bodies—to do otherwise is to disobey Him.

God has a plan for every aspect of your life, and His plan includes provisions for your spiritual, physical, and emotional health. But, He expects you to do your fair share of the work!

In a world that is chock-full of temptations, you may find it all too easy to make unhealthy choices. Your challenge, of course, is to resist those unhealthy temptations by every means you can, including prayer. And of this you can be sure: when you ask for God's help, He will give it.

The Basics:
What You Need to Know

One of the wisest choices you can make is the choice
to take care of your body. That means saying "Yes"
to a healthy lifestyle and "No" to any substance
that has the potential to harm you.

What the Bible Says

A cheerful disposition is good for your health;
gloom and doom leave you bone-tired.
Proverbs 17:22 MSG

Therefore, brothers, by the mercies of God,
I urge you to present your bodies as a living sacrifice,
holy and pleasing to God; this is your spiritual worship.
Romans 12:1 HCSB

They brought unto him all sick people that were
taken with diverse diseases and torments . . .
and he healed them.
Matthew 4:24 KJV

Big Ideas

Jesus Christ is the One by Whom, for Whom,
through Whom everything was made. Therefore,
He knows what's wrong in your life and how to fix it.

Anne Graham Lotz

God wants you to give Him your body.
Some people do foolish things with their bodies.
God wants your body as a holy sacrifice.

Warren Wiersbe

If you desire to improve your physical well-being
and your emotional outlook,
increasing your faith can help you.

John Maxwell

A Prayer for Today

Lord, when I am ill or weak or troubled
You heal me. Renew me, Father, and let me trust
Your will for my life. Let me welcome
Your unending love and Your healing touch,
now and forever.
Amen

CHAPTER 11

Choosing to Use Your Talent

I remind you to fan into flame the gift of God.
2 Timothy 1:6 NIV

Face it: you've got an array of talents that need to be refined. All people possess special gifts—bestowed from the Father above—and you are no exception. But, your particular gift is no guarantee of success; it must be cultivated—by you—or it will go unused . . . and God's gift to you will be squandered.

Are you willing to do the hard work that's required to discover your talents and to develop them? If you are wise, you'll answer "yes." After all, if you don't make the most of your talents, who has the most to lose? You do!

So make a promise to yourself that you will earnestly seek to discover the talents that God has given you. Then, nourish those talents and make them grow. Finally, vow to share your gifts with the world for as long as God gives you the power to do so. After all, the best way to say "Thank You" for God's gifts is to use them.

The Basics:
What You Need to Know

You have talents and opportunities which
you can choose to use . . . or not.
You must either use them or lose them.

What the Bible Says

*Now there are varieties of gifts, but the same Spirit.
And there are varieties of ministries, and the same Lord.*
1 Corinthians 12:4-5 NASB

*God has given gifts to each of you from his great
variety of spiritual gifts. Manage them well so that
God's generosity can flow through you.*
1 Peter 4:10 NLT

*The man who had received the five talents brought
the other five. "Master," he said, "you entrusted me
with five talents. See, I have gained five more."
His master replied, "Well done, good and faithful
servant! You have been faithful with a few things;
I will put you in charge of many things.
Come and share your master's happiness."*
Matthew 25:20-21 NIV

Big Ideas

What we are is God's gift to us.
What we become is our gift to God.

Anonymous

You are a unique blend of talents, skills,
and gifts, which makes you an indispensable
member of the body of Christ.

Charles Stanley

Not everyone possesses boundless energy or
a conspicuous talent. We are not equally blessed
with great intellect or physical beauty or emotional
strength. But we have all been given the same
ability to be faithful.

Gigi Graham Tchividjian

A Prayer for Today

Lord, You gave me talents and abilities for a reason.
Let me use my talents for the glory of Your kingdom,
and let me praise You always because
You are the Giver of all gifts, including mine.
Amen

CHAPTER 12

Choosing to Avoid All Those Temptations!

Put on the whole armor of God, that you may be able to stand against the wiles of the devil.

Ephesians 6:11 NKJV

ace facts: you live in a temptation-filled world. The devil is hard at work in your neighborhood, and so are his helpers. Here in the 21st-century, the bad guys are working around the clock to lead you astray. That's why you must remain vigilant.

In a letter to believers, Peter offers a stern warning: "Your adversary, the devil, prowls around like a roaring lion, seeking someone to devour" (1 Peter 5:8 NASB). What was true in New Testament times is equally true in our own. Satan tempts his prey and then devours them (and it's up to you—and only you—to make sure that you're not one of the ones being devoured!).

As a believer who seeks a radical relationship with Jesus, you must beware because temptations are everywhere. Satan is determined to win; you must be equally determined that he does not.

The Basics:
What You Need to Know

Temptations are everywhere.
It's your job to avoid them . . . or else!

What the Bible Says

*Be sober, be vigilant; because your adversary
the devil walks about like a roaring lion,
seeking whom he may devour.*
1 Peter 5:8 NKJV

*No temptation has seized you except what is
common to man. And God is faithful;
he will not let you be tempted beyond what you can
bear. But when you are tempted, he will also provide
a way out so that you can stand up under it.*
1 Corinthians 10:13 NIV

*The Lord knows how to deliver the godly
out of temptations.*
2 Peter 2:9 NKJV

Big Ideas

Our battles are first won or lost in the secret
places of our will in God's presence,
never in full view of the world.
Oswald Chambers

Flee temptation without leaving
a forwarding address.
Barbara Johnson

Jesus faced every temptation known to humanity
so that He could identify with us.
Beth Moore

A Prayer for Today

Dear Lord, help me to behave myself like
a faithful follower of Your Son. Let me keep
Christ in my heart, and let me put the devil in his place:
far away from me!
Amen

PRAYER

CHAPTER 13

Choosing to Talk Things Over with God

If you don't know what you're doing, pray to the Father. He loves to help. You'll get his help, and won't be condescended to when you ask for it. Ask boldly, believingly, without a second thought. People who "worry their prayers" are like wind-whipped waves. Don't think you're going to get anything from the Master that way, adrift at sea, keeping all your options open.

James 1:5-8 MSG

Are you faced with a difficult choice or an important decision? Then pray about it. If you talk to God sincerely and often, He won't lead you astray. Instead, God will guide you and help you make more intelligent choices . . . if you take the time to talk with Him.

If you have questions about whether you should do something or not, pray about it. If there is something you're worried about, ask God to comfort you. If you're having trouble with your relationships, ask God to help you sort things out. As you pray more, you'll discover that God is always near and that He's always ready to hear from you. So don't worry about things; pray about them. God is waiting . . . and listening!

The Basics:
What You Need to Know

When you have questions you can't answer,
prayer can help you answer them.

What the Bible Says

When a believing person prays, great things happen.
James 5:16 NCV

Rejoice always! Pray constantly.
Give thanks in everything, for this is God's will
for you in Christ Jesus.
1 Thessalonians 5:16-18 HCSB

Whatever you ask for in prayer, believe that you have
received it, and it will be yours.
Mark 11:24 NIV

Big Ideas

Prayer is the same as the breathing of air for the lungs.
Exhaling makes us get rid of our dirty air.
Inhaling gives clean air. To exhale is to confess,
to inhale is to be filled with the Holy Spirit.

Corrie ten Boom

Prayer accomplishes more than anything else.

Bill Bright

Avail yourself of the greatest privilege this side of
heaven: prayer. Jesus Christ died to make
this communion and communication with
the Father possible.

Billy Graham

A Prayer for Today

Lord, make me a prayerful Christian.
In good times and in bad times, in whatever state
I find myself, let me turn my prayers to You.
You always hear my prayers, God;
let me always pray them!
Amen

Choosing to Manage Your Time Wisely

*We can't afford to waste a minute, must not squander
these precious daylight hours in frivolity and indulgence,
in sleeping around and dissipation, in bickering and
grabbing everything in sight. Get out of bed and get
dressed! Don't loiter and linger, waiting until
the very last minute. Dress yourselves in Christ,
and be up and about!*

Romans 13:13-14 MSG

ime is a nonrenewable gift from God. But sometimes, we treat our time here on earth as if it were not a gift at all: We may be tempted to invest our lives in trivial pursuits and mindless diversions. But our Father in heaven wants us to do more . . . much more.

Are you one of those people who puts things off until the last minute? Do you waste time doing things that don't matter very much while putting off the important things until it's too late to do the job right? If so, it's now time to start making better choices.

It may seem like you've got all the time in the world to do the things you need to do, but time is shorter than you think. Time here on earth is limited . . . use it or lose it!

The Basics:
What You Need to Know

Every day, you get to choose how you will spend
your time. If you choose wisely,
you'll improve yourself and your life.

What the Bible Says

Hard work means prosperity;
only fools idle away their time.
Proverbs 12:11 NLT

Dear friends, don't let this one thing escape you:
with the Lord one day is like 1,000 years,
and 1,000 years like one day.
2 Peter 3:8 HCSB

So teach us to number our days,
that we may gain a heart of wisdom.
Psalm 90:12 NKJV

Big Ideas

The more time you give to something,
the more you reveal its importance
and value to you.

Rick Warren

Frustration is not the will of God.
There is time to do anything and everything
that God wants us to do.

Elisabeth Elliot

To choose time is to save time.

Francis Bacon

A Prayer for Today

Dear Lord, You have given me a wonderful gift:
time here on earth. Let me use it wisely—
for the glory of Your kingdom and the betterment
of Your world—today and every day.

Amen

CHAPTER 15

Getting Smarter Day by Day

When I was a child, I spoke and thought
and reasoned as a child does. But when I grew up,
I put away childish things.

1 Corinthians 13:11 NLT

A re you a fully-grown person? Physically: maybe so. But spiritually? No way! And thank goodness that you're not! Even if you're very mature for your age, you've still got lots of room to grow.

The 19th-century writer Hannah Whitall Smith observed, "The maturity of a Christian experience cannot be reached in a moment." No kidding. In truth, the search for spiritual growth lasts a lifetime.

When we cease to grow, either emotionally or spiritually, we do ourselves and our families a profound disservice. But, if we study God's Word, if we obey His commandments, and if we live in the center of His will, we will not be "stagnant" believers; we will, instead, be growing Christians . . . and that's exactly what God wants for our lives. Come to think of it, that's exactly what you should want, too.

The Basics:
What You Need to Know

Maturity means that you make wise choices.
Immaturity means that you continue making
unwise choices . . . it's as simple as that.

What the Bible Says

*So let us stop going over the basics of Christianity
again and again. Let us go on instead
and become mature in our understanding.*

Hebrews 6:1 NLT

*For this reason we also, since the day we heard it,
do not cease to pray for you, and to ask that you
may be filled with the knowledge of His will
in all wisdom and spiritual understanding.*

Colossians 1:9 NKJV

*Run away from infantile indulgence.
Run after mature righteousness—faith, love, peace—
joining those who are in honest
and serious prayer before God.*

2 Timothy 2:22 MSG

Big Ideas

I'm not what I want to be. I'm not what I'm going to be.
But, thank God, I'm not what I was!

Gloria Gaither

Being a Christian means accepting the terms of
creation, accepting God as our maker and redeemer,
and growing day by day into an increasingly
glorious creature in Christ, developing joy,
experiencing love, maturing in peace.

Eugene Peterson

When it comes to walking with God, there is
no such thing as instant maturity. God doesn't
mass produce His saints. He hand tools each one,
and it always takes longer than we expected.

Charles Swindoll

A Prayer for Today

Lord, let me grow in Your wisdom. When I study
Your Word and follow Your commandments,
I become a more mature Christian and a more effective
servant for You. Let me grow up, Lord, and let me keep
growing up every day that I live.
Amen

CHAPTER 16

Choosing to Serve

If they serve Him obediently, they will end their days in prosperity and their years in happiness.

Job 36:11 HCSB

f you genuinely want to make choices that are pleasing to God, you must ask yourself this question: "How does God want me to serve others?"

Whatever your age, wherever you happen to be, you may be certain of this: service to others is an integral part of God's plan for your life.

Every single day of your life, including this one, God will give you opportunities to serve Him by serving other people. Welcome those opportunities with open arms. They are God's gift to you, His way of allowing you to achieve greatness in His kingdom.

The Basics:
What You Need to Know

If you choose to serve, you'll be doing the world
(and yourself) a big favor.

What the Bible Says

There are different kinds of gifts, but they are all from the same Spirit. There are different ways to serve but the same Lord to serve.

1 Corinthians 12:4-5 NCV

So prepare your minds for service and have self-control. All your hope should be for the gift of grace that will be yours when Jesus Christ is shown to you.

1 Peter 1:13 NCV

Therefore, since we receive a kingdom which cannot be shaken, let us show gratitude, by which we may offer to God an acceptable service with reverence and awe . . . .

Hebrews 12:28 NASB

Big Ideas

Doing something positive toward another person is
a practical approach to feeling good about yourself.

Barbara Johnson

Through our service to others,
God wants to influence our world for Him.

Vonette Bright

Service is the pathway to real significance.

Rick Warren

A Prayer for Today

Dear Lord, let me help others in every way that I can.
Jesus served others; I can too. I will serve other people
with my good deeds and with my prayers.
And I will give thanks for everybody who helps me.
Amen

CHAPTER 17

Choosing to Be a Good Example

*We have around us many people whose lives tell us
what faith means. So let us run the race that is before
us and never give up. We should remove from our lives
anything that would get in the way and the sin
that so easily holds us back.*

Hebrews 12:1 NCV

Iow do people know that you're a Christian? Well, you can tell them, of course. And make no mistake about it: talking about your faith in God is a very good thing to do. But simply telling people about Jesus isn't enough. You must also be willing to show people how an extremely devoted Christian (like you) should behave.

Is your life a picture book of your creed? Do your actions line up with your beliefs? Are you willing to practice the philosophy that you preach? If so, congratulations. If not, it's time for a change.

Like it or not, your behavior is a powerful example to others. The question is not whether you will be an example to your family and friends; the question is what kind of example will you be?

Corrie ten Boom advised, "Don't worry about what you do not understand. Worry about what you do understand in the Bible but do not live by." And that's sound advice because your family and friends are always watching . . . and so, for that matter, is God.

The Basics:
What You Need to Know

You can choose to be a good example . . . or not.
The choice you make will have a big impact on
your own life and on the lives of others,
so choose carefully.

What the Bible Says

*In everything you do, stay away from complaining
and arguing, so that no one can speak a word of
blame against you. You are to live clean, innocent lives
as children of God in a dark world full of crooked
and perverse people. Let your lives shine
brightly before them.*
Philippians 2:14-15 NLT

*In every way be an example of doing good deeds.
When you teach, do it with honesty and seriousness.*
Titus 2:7 NCV

*You are the light that gives light to the world . . . .
In the same way, you should be a light for other people.
Live so that they will see the good things you do
and will praise your Father in heaven.*
Matthew 5:14,16 NCV

Big Ideas

"I read about it in the Bible" is true and good.
Yet, "I have seen him with the eyes of my heart"
is often more convincing. And convicting.

Liz Curtis Higgs

Our walk counts far more than our talk, always!

George Mueller

We can talk about faith, but what we live
shows the true faith behind the words.

Jay Kesler

A Prayer for Today

Dear Lord, help me be a worthy example to
my friends and to my family. Let the things that I say
and the things that I do show everyone
what it means to be a follower of Your Son.
Amen

CHAPTER 18

When You Make Unwise Choices

*If you hide your sins, you will not succeed.
If you confess and reject them,
you will receive mercy.*

Proverbs 28:13 NCV

When you make a mistake, do you get really mad at yourself . . . or maybe really, really, really mad? Hopefully not! After all, everybody makes mistakes, and nobody is expected to be perfect.

Even when you make mistakes, God loves you . . . so you should love yourself, too.

So the next time you make a mistake, make the smart choice: choose to learn from it. And after you've learned your lesson, try never to make that same mistake again. But don't be too hard on yourself. God doesn't expect you to be perfect, and since He loves you anyway, you should feel that way, too.

The Basics:
What You Need to Know

When you make mistakes (and you will) the best time
to fix those mistakes is now, not later.

What the Bible Says

You were taught, with regard to your former way of life, to put off your old self, which is being corrupted by its deceitful desires; to be made new in the attitude of your minds; and to put on the new self, created to be like God in true righteousness and holiness.

Ephesians 4:22-24 NIV

I waited patiently for the LORD; he turned to me and heard my cry. He lifted me out of the slimy pit, out of the mud and mire; he set my feet on a rock and gave me a firm place to stand. He put a new song in my mouth, a hymn of praise to our God . . . .

Psalm 40:1-3 NIV

If we confess our sins, he is faithful and just and will forgive us our sins and purify us from all unrighteousness.

1 John 1:9 NIV

Big Ideas

I hope you don't mind me telling you all this.
One can learn only by seeing one's mistakes.

C. S. Lewis

God is able to take mistakes, when they are
committed to Him, and make of them something for
our good and for His glory.

Ruth Bell Graham

Father, take our mistakes and turn them
into opportunities.

Max Lucado

A Prayer for Today

Dear Lord, there's a right way to do things
and a wrong way to do things. When I do things
that are wrong, help me be quick to ask for
forgiveness . . . and quick to correct my mistakes.
Amen

CHAPTER 19

Choosing to Follow Your Conscience

For indeed, the kingdom of God is within you.
Luke 17:21 NKJV

God gave you something called a conscience: some people describe it as a little voice, but really, it's a feeling—it's a feeling that tells you whether something is right or wrong. Your conscience will usually tell you what to do and when to do it. Pay attention to that feeling, and trust it.

If you choose to slow down and listen to your conscience, you'll usually stay out of trouble. And if you listen to your conscience, it won't be so hard to control your own behavior. Why? Because most of the time, your conscience already knows right from wrong. So don't be in such a hurry to do things. Instead of "jumping right in," listen to your conscience. In the end, you'll be very glad you did.

The Basics:
What You Need to Know

If you listen to your conscience,
you'll make better choices.
If you don't, you won't.

What the Bible Says

If then you were raised with Christ, seek those things which are above, where Christ is, sitting at the right hand of God. Set your mind on things above, not on things on the earth.

Colossians 3:1-2 NKJV

So I strive always to keep my conscience clear before God and man.

Acts 24:16 NIV

Let us come near to God with a sincere heart and a sure faith, because we have been made free from a guilty conscience, and our bodies have been washed with pure water.

Hebrews 10:22 NCV

Big Ideas

There is no pillow so soft as a clear conscience.

French Proverb

A good conscience is a continual feast.

Francis Bacon

The convicting work of the Holy Spirit awakens,
disturbs, and judges.

Franklin Graham

A Prayer for Today

Lord, You have given me a conscience that tells me
right from wrong. Let me listen to that quiet voice
so that I might do Your will and follow
Your Word today and every day.
Amen

CHAPTER 20

Choosing to Forgive

Be even-tempered, content with second place, quick to forgive an offense. Forgive as quickly and completely as the Master forgave you. And regardless of what else you put on, wear love. It's your basic, all-purpose garment. Never be without it.

Colossians 3:13-14 MSG

Are you the kind of guy or girl who has a tough time forgiving and forgetting? If so, welcome to the club. Most of us find it difficult to forgive the people who have hurt us. And that's too bad because life would be much simpler if we could forgive people "once and for all" and be done with it. Yet forgiveness is seldom that easy. Usually, the decision to forgive is straightforward, but the process of forgiving is more difficult. Forgiveness is a journey that requires effort, time, perseverance, and prayer.

If there exists even one person whom you have not forgiven (and that includes yourself), obey God's commandment: forgive that person today. And remember that bitterness, anger, and regret are not part of God's plan for your life. Forgiveness is.

If you sincerely wish to forgive someone, pray for that person. And then pray for yourself by asking God to heal your heart. Don't expect forgiveness to be easy or quick, but rest assured: with God as your partner, you can forgive . . . and you will.

The Basics: What You Need to Know

If you choose to forgive other people,
you're making the right choice.

What the Bible Says

*Our Father is kind; you be kind. "Don't pick on people,
jump on their failures, criticize their faults—unless,
of course, you want the same treatment. Don't condemn
those who are down; that hardness can boomerang.
Be easy on people; you'll find life a lot easier."*
Luke 6:36-37 MSG

Hatred stirs up trouble, but love forgives all wrongs.
Proverbs 10:12 NCV

*Be gentle with one another, sensitive.
Forgive one another as quickly and thoroughly
as God in Christ forgave you.*
Ephesians 4:32 MSG

Big Ideas

We are products of our past, but we don't
have to be prisoners of it. God specializes in
giving people a fresh start.

Rick Warren

Our Lord worked with people as they were,
and He was patient—not tolerant of sin,
but compassionate.

Vance Havner

God has been very gracious to me, for I never dwell
upon anything wrong which a person has done to me,
as to remember it afterwards. If I do remember it,
I always see some other virtue in the person.

St. Teresa of Avila

A Prayer for Today

Lord, just as You have forgiven me, I am going to forgive others. When I forgive others, I not only obey Your commandments, but I also free myself from bitterness and regret. Forgiveness is Your way, Lord, and I will make it my way, too.

Amen

CHAPTER 21

Choosing to Be Kind

And may the Lord make you increase and abound in love to one another and to all.

1 Thessalonians 3:12 NKJV

Kindness is a choice. Sometimes, when we feel happy or generous, we find it easy to be kind. Other times, when we are discouraged or tired, we can scarcely summon the energy to utter a single kind word. But, God's commandment is clear: He intends that we make the conscious choice to treat others with kindness and respect, no matter our circumstances, no matter our emotions.

In the busyness of daily life, it is easy to lose focus, and it is easy to become frustrated. When we are distracted or disappointed, we may neglect to share a kind word or a kind deed. This oversight hurts others, but it hurts us most of all.

Today, be alert for people who need your smile, your kind words, or your helping hand. Make kindness a centerpiece of your dealings with others. They will be blessed, and you will be too.

The Basics:
What You Need to Know

When you make the decision to be a genuinely
kind person, you'll make decisions that
improve your own life and the lives of
your family and friends.

What the Bible Says

Carry each other's burdens, and in this way you will fulfill the law of Christ.

Galatians 6:2 NIV

*Be kind to each other, tenderhearted,
forgiving one another, just as God
through Christ has forgiven you.*

Ephesians 4:32 NLT

*Finally, all of you should be of one mind,
full of sympathy toward each other, loving one another
with tender hearts and humble minds.*

1 Peter 3:8 NLT

Big Ideas

When you extend hospitality to others,
you're not trying to impress people,
you're trying to reflect God to them.

Max Lucado

When you launch an act of kindness
out into the crosswinds of life,
it will blow kindness back to you.

Dennis Swanberg

A little kindly advice is better than
a great deal of scolding.

Fanny Crosby

A Prayer for Today

Lord, make me a loving, encouraging Christian.
And, let my love for Christ be reflected through
the kindness that I show to those who need
the healing touch of the Master's hand.
Amen

CHAPTER 22

Choosing to Control Your Temper

*I want men everywhere to lift up holy hands in prayer,
without anger or disputing.*
1 Timothy 2:8 NIV

The frustrations of everyday living can sometimes get the better of us, and we allow minor disappointments to cause us major problems. When we allow ourselves to become overly irritated by the inevitable ups and downs of life, we become overstressed, overheated, over-anxious, and just plain angry.

As the old saying goes, "Anger usually improves nothing but the arch of a cat's back." So don't allow feelings of anger or frustration to rule your life, or, for that matter, your day—your life is simply too short for that, and you deserve much better treatment than that . . . from yourself.

The Basics:
What You Need to Know

When you lose your temper . . . you lose.

What the Bible Says

Everyone should be quick to listen, slow to speak and slow to become angry, for man's anger does not bring about the righteous life that God desires.

James 1:19-20 NIV

When you are angry, do not sin, and be sure to stop being angry before the end of the day.
Do not give the devil a way to defeat you.

Ephesians 4:26-27 NCV

But I tell you that men will have to give account on the day of judgment for every careless word they have spoken. For by your words you will be acquitted, and by your words you will be condemned.

Matthew 12:36-37 NIV

Big Ideas

Life is too short to spend it being angry, bored, or dull.

Barbara Johnson

Anger unresolved will only bring you woe.

Kay Arthur

When you strike out in anger, you may miss
the other person, but you will always hit yourself.

Jim Gallery

A Prayer for Today

Dear Lord, help me to turn away from
angry thoughts and angry people. Help me always
to use Jesus as my guide for life, and let me trust
His promises today and forever.
Amen

Avoiding the Trap of Materialism

And He told them, "Watch out and be on guard
against all greed, because one's life is not in
the abundance of his possessions."
Luke 12:15 HCSB

Are you overly concerned with the stuff that money can buy? If so, here's a word of warning: your love for material possessions is getting in the way of your relationship with God.

Up on the stage of life, material possessions should play a rather small role. Of course, we all need the basic necessities like food, clothing, and a place to live. But once we've met those needs, the piling up of possessions creates more problems than it solves. Our real riches, of course, are not of this world. We're never really rich until we are rich in spirit.

Our society is in love with money and the things that money can buy. God is not. God cares about people, not possessions, and so must we. We must, to the best of our abilities, love our neighbors as ourselves, and we must, to the best of our abilities, resist the mighty temptation to place possessions ahead of people.

Money, in and of itself, is not evil; worshipping money is. So today, as you seek better ways to know your Creator, remember that God is almighty, but the dollar is not.

The Basics:
What You Need to Know

If you choose to allow material possessions to rule
your life, you're making a big mistake.

What the Bible Says

No one can serve two masters. The person will hate one master and love the other, or will follow one master and refuse to follow the other. You cannot serve both God and worldly riches.

Matthew 6:24 NCV

He who trusts in his riches will fall,
but the righteous will flourish . . . .

Proverbs 11:28 NKJV

For the mind-set of the flesh is death,
but the mind-set of the Spirit is life and peace.

Romans 8:6 HCSB

Big Ideas

Greed is enslaving. The more you have,
the more you want—until eventually
avarice consumes you.

Kay Arthur

As faithful stewards of what we have,
ought we not to give earnest thought to
our staggering surplus?

Elisabeth Elliot

The cross is laid on every Christian.
It begins with the call to abandon
the attachments of this world.

Dietrich Bonhoeffer

A Prayer for Today

Dear Lord, help me remember that the things in this
world that are really valuable are my life,
my family, and my relationship with You.
Amen

CHAPTER 24

God's Word Can Help You Make Wise Choices

For the word of God is living and effective and sharper than any two-edged sword, penetrating as far as to divide soul, spirit, joints, and marrow; it is a judge of the ideas and thoughts of the heart.

Hebrews 4:12 HCSB

God's Word is unlike any other book. The words of Matthew 4:4 remind us that, "Man shall not live by bread alone but by every word that proceedeth out of the mouth of God" (KJV). As believers, we are instructed to study the Bible and meditate upon its meaning for our lives, yet far too many Bibles are laid aside by well-intentioned believers who would like to study the Bible if they could "just find the time."

Warren Wiersbe observed, "When the child of God looks into the Word of God, he sees the Son of God. And, he is transformed by the Spirit of God to share in the glory of God." God's Holy Word is, indeed, a transforming, life-changing, one-of-a-kind treasure. And it's up to you—and only you—to use it that way.

The Basics:
What You Need to Know

If you study the Bible every day,
you'll learn how to live a better life
and how to make better choices.

What the Bible Says

But the word of the Lord endures forever. And this is the word that was preached as the gospel to you.
1 Peter 1:25 HCSB

Heaven and earth will pass away,
but My words will never pass away.
Matthew 24:35 HCSB

All Scripture is inspired by God and is profitable for teaching, for rebuking, for correcting, for training in righteousness, so that the man of God may be complete, equipped for every good work.
2 Timothy 3:16-17 HCSB

Big Ideas

Weave the unveiling fabric of God's word through
your heart and mind. It will hold strong,
even if the rest of life unravels.

Gigi Graham Tchividjian

Meditating upon His Word will inevitably bring
peace of mind, strength of purpose,
and power for living.

Bill Bright

Faith is the virtue that enables us to believe and obey
the Word of God, for faith comes from hearing and
hearing from the Word of God (Romans 10:17).

Franklin Graham

A Prayer for Today

Heavenly Father, Your Holy Word is a light unto the world; let me study it, trust it, and share it with all who cross my path. In all that I do, help me be a worthy witness for You as I share the Good News of Your perfect Son and Your perfect Word.

Amen

CHAPTER 25

Choosing to Avoid the Media Hype

Let no one deceive himself. If anyone among you seems to be wise in this age, let him become a fool that he may become wise. For the wisdom of this world is foolishness with God. For it is written, "He catches the wise in their own craftiness."

1 Corinthians 3:18-19 NKJV

ometimes it's hard being a Christian, especially when the world keeps pumping out messages that are contrary to your faith.

The media is working around the clock in an attempt to rearrange your priorities. The media says that your appearance is all-important, that your clothes are all-important, that your car is all-important, and that partying is all-important. But guess what? Those messages are lies. The important things in your life have little to do with parties or appearances. The all-important things in life have to do with your faith, your family, and your future. Period.

Are you willing to stand up for your faith? If so, you'll be doing yourself a king-sized favor. And consider this: When you begin to speak up for God, isn't it logical to assume that you'll also begin to know Him in a more meaningful way? Of course you will.

So do yourself a favor: forget the media hype, and pay attention to God. Stand up for Him and be counted, not just in church where it's relatively easy to be a Christian, but also outside the church, where it's significantly harder. You owe it to God . . . and you owe it to yourself.

The Basics:
What You Need to Know

The media is sending out messages that are dangerous
to your physical, emotional, and spiritual health.
If you choose to believe those messages,
you're setting yourself up for lots of trouble.

What the Bible Says

*For whatever is born of God overcomes the world.
And this is the victory that has overcome the world—
our faith.*

1 John 5:4 NKJV

*Do not love the world or the things in the world.
If you love the world,
the love of the Father is not in you.*

1 John 2:15 NCV

*Religion that God our Father accepts as pure
and faultless is this: to look after orphans and
widows in their distress and to keep oneself
from being polluted by the world.*

James 1:27 NIV

Big Ideas

I have a divided heart, trying to love God and the world
at the same time. God says, "You can't love me
as you should if you love this world too."

Mary Morrison Suggs

The only ultimate disaster that can befall us,
I have come to realize, is to feel ourselves
to be home on earth.

Max Lucado

Every Christian is a contradiction to this old world.
He crosses it at every point. He goes against the grain
from beginning to end. From the day that he is born
again until the day that he goes on to be with the Lord,
he must stand against the current of a world
always going the other way.

Vance Havner

A Prayer for Today

Lord, this world is a crazy place, and I have many
opportunities to stray from Your commandments.
Help me learn to obey You! Let me keep Christ
in my heart, and let me put the devil in his place:
far away from me!
Amen

The Best Time to Choose

"I say this because I know what I am planning for you,"
says the Lord. "I have good plans for you, not plans to
hurt you. I will give you hope and a good future."

Jeremiah 29:11 NCV

aybe you've heard this old saying: "Look before you leap." Well, that saying may be old, but it still applies to you. Before you jump into something, you should look ahead and plan ahead. Otherwise, you might soon be sorry you jumped!

When you acquire the habit of planning ahead, you'll usually make better choices. So when it comes to the important things in life, make a plan and stick to it. When you do, you'll think about the consequences of your actions before you do something silly . . . or dangerous . . . or both.

The Basics:
What You Need to Know

The best time to decide how you're going
to behave is before you find yourself in a difficult
(or tempting) situation. So think ahead,
plan ahead, and follow your plan!

What the Bible Says

Let your eyes look forward;
fix your gaze straight ahead.
Proverbs 4:25 HCSB

Careful planning puts you ahead in the long run;
hurry and scurry puts you further behind.
Proverbs 21:5 MSG

But a noble person plans noble things;
he stands up for noble causes.
Isaiah 32:8 HCSB

Big Ideas

Plan ahead—it wasn't raining when Noah built the ark.

Anonymous

The only way you can experience abundant life is to
surrender your plans to Him.

Charles Stanley

Allow your dreams a place in your prayers and plans.
God-given dreams can help you move into
the future He is preparing for you.

Barbara Johnson

A Prayer for Today

Dear Lord, give me the wisdom to accept the past
and the insight to plan for the future.
And help me align my plans with Your plans,
Father, this day and every day.
Amen

CHAPTER 27

Choosing to Control Yourself

Knowing God leads to self-control.
Self-control leads to patient endurance,
and patient endurance leads to godliness.

2 Peter 1:6 NLT

Would you like a winning formula for making smart choices? Think about things first and do things next, not vice versa.

Are you, at times, just a little bit too impulsive? Do you react first and think about your reaction second? If so, God wants to have a little chat with you.

God's Word is clear: as a believer, you are called to lead a life of discipline, diligence, moderation, and maturity. But the world often tempts you to behave otherwise. Everywhere you turn, or so it seems, you are encouraged to give in to any number of powerful temptations. So you should plan on being tempted . . . and you should plan on saying, "No!"

The Basics:
What You Need to Know

If you're too impulsive, you'll make unwise choices,
so when in doubt, slow down.

What the Bible Says

*So prepare your minds for service
and have self-control.*
1 Peter 1:13 NCV

*All athletes practice strict self-control.
They do it to win a prize that will fade away,
but we do it for an eternal prize.*
1 Corinthians 9:25 NLT

*Learn the truth and never reject it.
Get wisdom, self-control, and understanding.*
Proverbs 23:23 NCV

Big Ideas

Man's great danger is the combination of
his increased control over the elements and
his lack of control over himself.

Albert Schweitzer

Love, joy, peace, patience, kindness, goodness,
faithfulness, gentleness, and self-control. To these
I commit my day. If I succeed, I will give thanks.
If I fail, I will seek his grace. And then, when this day is
done, I will place my head on my pillow and rest.

Max Lucado

The effective Christians of history have been men and
women of great personal discipline—mental discipline,
discipline of the body, discipline of the tongue,
and discipline of the emotion.

Billy Graham

A Prayer for Today

Dear God, today I will slow down and think about things before I do them. And when I slow down to think about things, I will always try to do what's right.

Amen

CHAPTER 28

Choosing to Be Yourself

You made all the delicate, inner parts of my body and knit me together in my mother's womb. Thank you for making me so wonderfully complex! Your workmanship is marvelous—and how well I know it.

Psalm 139:13-14 NLT

When you feel better about yourself, you make better choices. But sometimes, it's hard to feel good about yourself, especially when you live in a society that keeps sending out the message that you've got to be perfect.

Are you your own worst critic? And in response to that criticism, are you constantly trying to transform yourself into a person who meets society's expectations, but not God's expectations? If so, it's time to become a little more understanding of the person you see whenever you look into the mirror.

Millions of words have been written about various ways to improve self-esteem. Yet, maintaining a healthy self-image is, to a surprising extent, a matter of doing three things:

1. Obeying God
2. Thinking healthy thoughts
3. Finding things to do that please your Creator and yourself.

When you concentrate on these things, your self-image will tend to take care of itself.

The Basics:
What You Need to Know

When you learn to accept yourself,
imperfections and all,
you'll make better choices.

What the Bible Says

*For everything created by God is good,
and nothing should be rejected
if it is received with thanksgiving.*

1 Timothy 4:4 HCSB

*A man's heart plans his way,
but the LORD determines his steps.*

Proverbs 16:9 HCSB

*Should we accept only good from God
and not adversity?*

Job 2:10 HCSB

Big Ideas

Find satisfaction in him who made you,
and only then find satisfaction in yourself
as part of his creation.

St. Augustine

The meek man is not a human mouse afflicted
with a sense of his own inferiority. Rather he may
be in his moral life as bold as a lion and as strong
as Samson; but he has stopped being fooled about
himself. He has accepted God's estimate of his own
life. He knows he is as weak and helpless as God
declared him to be, but paradoxically, he knows at
the same time that he is in the sight of God of more
importance than angels. In himself, nothing;
in God, everything. That is his motto.

A. W. Tozer

A Prayer for Today

Lord, I have so much to learn and so many ways to
improve myself, but You love me just as I am.
Thank You for Your love and for Your Son.
And, help me to become the person that
You want me to become.
Amen

CHAPTER 29

Choosing to Stand Up for Your Beliefs

All things are possible for the one who believes.
Mark 9:23 NCV

If you're willing to stand up for the things you believe in, you'll make better choices. But if you're one person on Sunday morning and a different person throughout the rest of the week, you'll be doing yourself—and your conscience—a big disservice.

The moment that you decide to stand up for your beliefs, you can no longer be a lukewarm, halfhearted Christian. And, when you are no longer a lukewarm Christian, God rejoices (and the devil doesn't).

So stand up for your beliefs. And remember this: in the battle of good versus evil, the devil never takes a day off . . . and neither should you.

The Basics:
What You Need to Know

When you stand up for your beliefs,
you'll make better choices.

What the Bible Says

I know whom I have believed and am persuaded that He is able to guard what has been entrusted to me until that day.
2 Timothy 1:12 HCSB

Everyone who believes that Jesus is the Messiah has been born of God, and everyone who loves the parent also loves his child.
1 John 5:1 HCSB

Then He said to Thomas, "Put your finger here and observe My hands. Reach out your hand and put it into My side. Don't be an unbeliever, but a believer."
John 20:27 HCSB

Big Ideas

Jesus taught that the evidence that confirms
our leaps of faith comes after we risk believing,
not before.

Gloria Gaither

What I believe about God is the most
important thing about me.

A. W. Tozer

God's presence is with you, but you have to make
a choice to believe—and I mean, really believe—
that this is true. This conscious decision is yours alone.

Bill Hybels

A Prayer for Today

Heavenly Father, I believe in You, and I believe in
Your Word. Help me to live in such a way that
my actions validate my beliefs—
and let the glory be Yours forever.
Amen

CHAPTER 30

The Ultimate Choice

For God so loved the world that He gave His only begotten Son, that whoever believes in Him should not perish but have everlasting life.

John 3:16 NKJV

Your ability to envision the future, like your life here on earth, is limited. God's vision, however, is not burdened by any such limitations. He sees all things, He knows all things, and His plans for you extend throughout eternity.

God's plans are not limited to the events of daily life. Your Heavenly Father has bigger things in mind for you . . . much bigger things. So praise the Creator for the gift of eternal life and share the Good News with all who cross your path. And remember: if you have given your heart to the Son, you belong to the Father—today, tomorrow, and for all eternity.

The Basics:
What You Need to Know

The ultimate choice for you is the choice to invite God's Son into your heart.

What the Bible Says

Just then someone came up and asked Him, "Teacher, what good must I do to have eternal life?" "Why do you ask Me about what is good?" He said to him. "There is only One who is good. If you want to enter into life, keep the commandments."

Matthew 19:16-17 HCSB

And this is the testimony: God has given us eternal life, and this life is in His Son. The one who has the Son has life. The one who doesn't have the Son of God does not have life.

1 John 5:11-12 HCSB

I have written these things to you who believe in the name of the Son of God, so that you may know that you have eternal life.

1 John 5:13 HCSB

Big Ideas

If you are a believer, your judgment will not determine your eternal destiny. Christ's finished work on Calvary was applied to you the moment you accepted Christ as Savior.

Beth Moore

Those of us who know the wonderful grace of redemption look forward to an eternity with God, when all things will be made new, when all our longings will at last find ultimate and final satisfaction.

Joseph Stowell

God loves you and wants you to experience peace and life—abundant and eternal.

Billy Graham

A Prayer for Today

Lord, You have given me the gift of eternal life through
Christ Jesus. I praise You for that priceless gift.
Because I am saved, I will share the story of
Your Son and the glory of my salvation with a world
that desperately needs Your grace.
Amen

Bible Verses
to Memorize

Be strong and brave, and do the work.
Don't be afraid or discouraged,
because the Lord God,
my God, is with you.
He will not fail you or leave you.

1 Chronicles 28:20 NCV

Therefore, brothers, by the mercies
of God, I urge you to present
your bodies as a living sacrifice,
holy and pleasing to God;
this is your spiritual worship.

Romans 12:1 HCSB

For to me to live is Christ,
and to die is gain.

Philippians 1:21 KJV

Be kind to each other, tenderhearted, forgiving one another, just as God through Christ has forgiven you.

Ephesians 4:32 NLT

Who can separate us from the love of Christ? Can affliction or anguish or persecution or famine or nakedness or danger or sword? . . . No, in all these things we are more than victorious through Him who loved us.

Romans 8:35,37 HCSB

But the word of the Lord endures forever. And this is the word that was preached as the gospel to you.

1 Peter 1:25 HCSB

But God demonstrates His own love toward us, in that while we were still sinners, Christ died for us.

Romans 5:8 NKJV

I know whom I have believed
and am persuaded that
He is able to guard what
has been entrusted to me
until that day.

2 Timothy 1:12 HCSB

For where two or three come together in my name, there am I with them.

Matthew 18:20 NIV

Be hospitable to one another without complaining.

1 Peter 4:9 HCSB

If we confess our sins, He is faithful and
righteous to forgive us our sins and
to cleanse us from all unrighteousness.

1 John 1:9 HCSB

All Scripture is inspired by God
and is profitable for teaching,
for rebuking, for correcting,
for training in righteousness, so that
the man of God may be complete,
equipped for every good work.

2 Timothy 3:16-17 HCSB

I have learned,
in whatsoever state I am,
therewith to be content.

Philippians 4:11 KJV

A man's heart plans his way,
but the Lord determines
his steps.

Proverbs 16:9 HCSB

Therefore, if anyone is in Christ,
he is a new creation;
the old has gone,
the new has come!

2 Corinthians 5:17 NIV

We must obey God rather than men.

Acts 5:29 HCSB

For God so loved
the world that He gave
His only begotten Son,
that whoever believes
in Him should not perish
but have everlasting life.

John 3:16 NKJV